HOW TO MAKE MONEY ONLINE
WHEN YOU'RE OVER 50

Internet Business Ideas

By PEGGY HATCHET

Table of Contents

Foreword

There are many books on the subject of *making money on the Internet*. Like many of you, I started reading my share of them; some I immediately put down and others were commonplace.

Most of them are full of overly fluffed statistics, inflated promises--and just plain ole lies. It's an embarrassment to genuine writers who base their manuscripts on actual research. But I digress.

The truth is there are no easily made millions. In fact, it's not easy to toil on a nine to five every day and then have to wait until the end of the week to get paid. There's nothing easy about that. So, if it's that hard on a small level, you can imagine the sweat that goes into making millions.

Unless you have a Facebook idea, it's time to grind and get to work on your passionate desire for wealth.

Even Mark Zukerburg pulled down countless hours of experimenting with hypertext markup language, or HTML. He didn't wake up one day a millionaire. His success is the sum of his passion, his vision and determination to see it through, even when he wanted to give up.

Many factors can kill the passion for a dream. One of the most common hinders is the way we think about *aging*.

Without realizing it, we place a time limit on success and deny ourselves the ultimate accomplishment.

Everywhere you turn somebody is saying you've missed your opportunity if you don't do it before age 40.

That's just a bunch of powerless words... that is, unless you believe them.

The amazing thing about making money on the Internet is you can do it anywhere. And if you're over 40, don't worry, you can sit down.

And I digress again.

The first thing you want to do is get your mind right. No amount of success flows through a cloudy, negative mind. If you believe you're too old to embark on the path to achieve your financial dreams, close this page. You beliefs override the possibility of achievement. Get your mind right!

The second thing you have to do, after you get your mind right, is to work your passion, because passion gives life to your dream when everyone else tells you it's too late.

In other words, you may be over 50 and taking two or three different medications, but so what? You're still alive. Work your passion.

There are millions to be made on the Internet. Zuckerburg and others like him are evidence of that.

On a smaller scale, there are thousands who make 50 thousand a year or more. However, you must keep in mind that it wasn't overnight, it wasn't easy and it wasn't too good to be true. They simply had a passion, they believed they could realize their dream and they did the work.

With this book, I hope to show you that it is never too late to achieve a goal. Even when you die, you should *die trying to live.*

I want to show you that there is something for you to do when everyone says it's over. I want to show you that as long as you're breathing, it's never over--unless you decide it's over. I want to encourage you to get up off the couch and flex your intelligence. Grab hold of that inspiration and put the gleam back in your eye.

This book is called *How to Make Money Online When You're Over 50*. However, these things are not limited to an age group. I selected this age because of the stereotype that says *a person waited too late if they're over fifty*.

Okay. Let's go. Let's take this journey!
Happy trails,

DEDICATION

To all my over-50 peers, here's to your success.

WHAT'S AGE GOT TO DO WITH IT ANYWAY?

"If you fail to plan, you plan to fail."

Over 50 and Hating It

In the average mind, age has everything to do with it. For the above-average mind, age is a benefit--with one condition. To benefit from age, physical health must be optimal. Otherwise, who can profit from age, while in a sickly, diseased body?

No one has yet explained what it is about reaching the 50-year-old mark that causes subconscious hysteria. For me, it didn't matter. I don't count years as they fall on my day of birth.

We really only have one birthday, and that's the day we're born. Everything after that is insignificant formality. That's not to say it's wrong to celebrate a day that represents your birth. But you have to admit, too much emphasis on the birthday concept just makes you more age conscious.

No one wants to hit the *fifty* mark. It's the age you technically stop being a *young adult*. Perhaps that has something to do with it.

The body really doesn't experience any noticeable changes at forty. At that age, all changes are in silent mode. You don't notice them right away, so you think you're one of the *blessed few* who seem to never age--until you hit fifty.

We're going through the preliminaries because it's helpful to know why we stop pursuing our goals at a certain age.

There isn't a law or specific protocol that says *don't actively pursue goals after reaching age fifty*. Most of us have a built-in age sensor that shuts down success pursuits when we reach the targeted birthday.

Hating life after reaching a certain age is learned behavior or a set of values given to us by cultural practice. This type of thinking is for the *ordinary* individual who follows the crowd over the cliff. Though we go through the motions of daily routine, every retiree has been heading toward that cliff of *mediocrity*. Whether we're fifteen or fifty, life is to be loved and lived--not hated and abandoned. Age amounts to knowledge and experience, and you need both to achieve any and all worthwhile endeavors.

50 is the Ultimate ~"F"~ Word, in terms of age; and making 50k in six months is the ultimate dream realization, when you can earn it by implementing your own creative idea, rather than with physical brokenness and stress.

A profitable niche website is one that solves a problem or answers a question or provide a specific service.

Thousands of people operate websites that are nothing more than a waste of time and money. They pay to host a site that's using web space and nothing more.

They have ads all over the place, in no particular order. The content is carelessly plastered in kindergarten fashion, and they have the nerve to ask you to *subscribe*.

What's even more bizarre is the fact that people actually subscribe to this annoying webite. Why? Because they offer something worth knowing about.

We've established that a person can literally throw something together, put it on the web and somebody will be interested in it.

What if you wrote out your creative plan, researched your idea and put together a spectacular website for it? If people can literally submit crap on the web and call it a site, then surely, you can submit a polished web page that gives people what they need or want.

A niche website MUST be unique and exclusive, even if there are already hundreds of sites on the subject.

To create a successful moneymaking niche site requires more than a great idea. Internet entrepreneurs have to do a lot of preliminary research. You have to have a clear vision of implementation before you begin.

For example, in order for a niche on *caring for newborns* to be successful, it would need to focus on a specific infancy attribute such as *grooming newborns to be geniuses*. Then you would include information on the types of music that promotes high IQ's, for instance.

Profitable niches are narrowed to mastering a single focus. This lends an expert feel to the project. A professional approach is only possible with a targeted approach. Broad subjects contain no expert appeal, as they are of the generalized dictionary feel, which lacks focused authority on the topic.

Moneymaking niche sites require a professional domain and site hosting.

When testing the Internet moneymaking climate, I began with a free hosting site. My domain name looked like this: *mysitename.wix.com*. This doesn't cut it. Period.

It's a turn-off for any business venture that appears to be on welfare. No disrespect to welfare recipients. I'm merely making the point that business ventures must first **look profitable**, before they can actually **be profitable**.

Positive Thinking

#1

The people I talk to absolutely love this niche and so will you! There's so much that goes into this topic that the information is never boring.

You could begin by researching different publications and websites on the subject. See what areas are not covered as much and choose a niche in that area.

For instance, many books on positive thinking address the power of positive thinking; overcoming negative thinking; and the stress factor. However, not many books or websites focus on how thinking affects longevity.

Choosing this niche is worth it, if you're willing to do the leg work. Leg work is not specific to this niche alone. We have to be willing to do the work in any endeavor.

While reading different books on the subject and scanning various websites as part of your research, you might just reform your own thinking!

You get a two-for-one. Wouldn't that be grand? *Success is the sweet reward of hard work.*

Those who can, do; those who can't, teach; and those who can do neither, administer.

Ways to Relieve Stress

#2

All of us have a little or a lot of stress that we want to be rid of. We just have no idea how to enjoy doing it. *Humans have to enjoy a process if they are to continue it.*

Think about some things you would enjoy doing as part of a stress-relieving process.
- schedule an annual retreat
- weekly online round-tables to interact and *empty out*
- solicit stories about what caused personal stress, how they conquered it; what they reccommend, etc. Choose a story to feature weekly, bi-weekly or monthly (depending on the number of stories)

You may think this topic to be overworked, and any information you present would be repetitive. If you don't thoroughly research it and creatively think it through, it will. This niche is dying for some creative delivery!

Enough with all the medical jargon about what stress does to the body. It's important. But we know it by heart. Talk about how relieving stress can be fun and exciting.

Offer online stress-relieving training techniques; have video conferences; have an interactive website that gets your subscribers involved.

Got it?

Luck is infatuated with the efficient.

Maintaining a Healthy Heart

#3

This is another niche subject that's widely popular. Medical clinics pass out pamphlets; community organizations offer workshops; many eat-healthy efforts inundate the atmosphere, and yet, all the delivery does is frighten people.

Again, the website has to be unique and fresh!

If you can find an interesting and appealing method of delivery, this is a great online niche.

Remember, the moment you have an idea, it's new and it's yours. But if you procrastinate or dismiss it, you'll look up one day and see it being implemented by someone else.

If you live a lifestyle that promotes heart health and it's something you're passionate about, throw your hat in the Internet ring! Nothing draws interest more than a success story.

However, if you're approaching it from the medical research angle, IT MUST HAVE SUPERB CONTENT AND UNIQUE DELIVERY. Otherwise, you'll have just another poorly implemented idea.

For all business ventures, patience is a necessary quality.

How To Remain Young at Heart

#4

In their heart, everybody wants to hold on to the energy and the vibrance of youth, whether they admit it or not. Youthfulness is bliss.

No. It doesn't mean you want to service people who deny the reality of aging. However, is does say that you want to help them maintain that part of themselves and not live in the dread of growing old and incapacitated.

This niche will attract millions of followers and/or subscribers because it speaks to what's important to them. Online Business ventures fail mostly because the niche wasn't that important to people, according to a survey of those exiting the subscription.

Sharing information with your subscribers about how they can remain young at heart will never get old or lose its appeal. Why? Because it's important to 100% of the population at some point in their life.

Depending on the type of setup you use, this website niche could easily be sold for millions.

How old are you 40-something, 50-something, 60-something or more? It doesn't matter. If you possess intelligence and have some spunk and desire, you can achieve what you will at ANY age.

One man's wage rise is another man's price increase. Costs always rise with wages.
You would think they've made enough money that they could afford to give the little man, who made them so big, a few more dollars

Personal Maintenance

#5

Anything that feeds *ego* or *vanity* will always be popular with the masses. Everyone is a little vain, some a lot. And many of us are egotistical to some degree. But that's alright.

Civilized people care about how they look, how well they do in a process, and how physically appealing they are. Caring about personal maintenance is a daily routine.

Everyone looks into the mirror and grooms themselves on a daily basis as part of their day-to-day schedule. We are preparing for work, school or some other appointment; grooming is part of that method. We want to look good, and when we do, we naturally feel good.

Having a unique personal maintenance niche website is a sound business choice and will never lack client enthusiasm--as long as you consistently provide a unique service, with fresh content and dynamic personal protocol. With these elements, there's no reason why this venture would fail, unless of course, the drive isn't there to work it until it's strong enough to work for itself.

This niche draws advertising from gyms, health-food stores, athletic supply companies, etc. Great income possibilities await the launching and cultivating of a personal maintenance site.

Going to work for a large company is like riding a train. Are you going sixty miles an hour or is the train going sixty miles an hour and you're sitting still?

For Those Who Say Manual Labor is the Only Way

This take on the subject refers specifically to observations that stipulate manual labor as the only legitimate way to earn money. On the other hand, physical work is no less important. In fact, manual labor built this country and made it the great nation that it is. And the human existence will never be without it.

Having said that, it would be closed-minded to categorize Internet-based work as illegitimate and insignificant. Unfortunately, no matter how legitimate or how lucrative an online business may be, because we don't understand the computing concept, we stereotype the Internet as a *bad place*.

Yes. Some people use the Internet to snare others, and we view doing business online negatively. However, we can say the same about being mugged while getting out of the car in the driveway. Does that mean your driveway is a bad place? No. Being mugged in your driveway opened your eyes, and made you more alert to your surroundings. The Internet is no different. If we have a bad online experience, it makes us wiser in our online behavior.

According to Forbes Magazine, Internet entrepreneurs generated over three billion dollars in 2010. That number is sure to have risen over the years.

I'm sure many of you will remain skeptical of doing business online. And it's okay to not want to do something. However, it is not okay to judge and marginalize someone else's efforts, because they happen to be different than yours.

This is for those of you who want to put your creative ideas to work for you after retirement, and are open to giving making a relaxed income a try. If you work at making your niche site the best it can be, it will work for you!

If a cluttered desk indicates a cluttered mind, what does an empty desk indicate?

Living a Pain-free Life

#6

Society is trained to need a pill to get up on, one to make it through the day and a pill to go to bed on.

However, the public is more conscious about the addiction dangers associated with taking prescription medication. More importantly, pain pills are extremely addictive; and if there's a site that promotes a pain-free life, yippee!

A site promoting methods for living pain-free will at least get curiosity traffic. And if the site is spectacular enough, curiosity traffic will convert into loyal subscribers.

The point of creating a niche site is to provide a service, answer a question, solve a problem, etc. Your site must do one or more of these things to generate money. Otherwise, it'll be just another mediocre site on the web.

Research, creative organization and delivery are key factors for any profitable site, but especially for one dealing with human physiology. In today's world, pharmaceutical remedy has created drug addicts of all ages. Ways to live pain free minus the pill-popping would attract a fair amount of regulars to the site.

Today's sales should be better than yesterday's and worse than tomorrow's.

Online Business Revenue Supplements Retirement

IRS records for 1999 list the highest and the lowest annual Internet income for ages 55-64. The highest was $61, 347; $27, 251 was recorded as the lowest.

A retiree no longer has to spend their days on the golf course doing the same boring thing with the same boring people. They don't have to feel like life is over because they retired.

Actually, they just changed schedules and locations. They still get up every morning at six o'clock. But instead of taking the subway or a taxi to uptown Manhattan, they're looking for another routine to fill their day.

If a creative idea doesn't kick in, most retirees find themselves in a ho-hum routine. Before long, they'bored and overweight. *How to Make Money Online When You're Over 50* offers legitimate alternatives to letting yourself go. Plus, you earn a pretty hefty annual supplement.

Realistically, the revenue from your niche website may trickle in before gaining enough traction to be viable. Being a retiree puts you in a great position; you're only losing seven or eight bucks a month for website hosting. I would guess you spend ten times that on recreational past time.

The point is, why not give it a try?

Find a topic or niche you're familiar with, a field you worked in or a hobby, like stamp collecting. Research the web to determine the best competitive edge. Decide how to deliver your idea, what type of site (membership, subscription, etc.) Write a detailed plan.

It's good to build your idea around what excites you. If it excites you, it's sure to excite your subscribers.

Peggy Hatchet

Business is more exciting than any game.

How to Build a Deck

#7

Any home improvement niche is popular with homeowners. Focusing on specific areas would serve better, as home improvement sites are popular and plentiful.

Choosing an area like deck-building is good, however, it's better to couple this particular niche with something like *best low-maintenance patio plants* or *pros and cons: enclosed patio vs. open layout*.

Many sites talk about do-it-yourself deck-building. So you won't have the niche exclusively. A fair number of them have step-by-step photos of the building process. Therefore, adding relevant subcategories like the ones mentioned above would separate your site from others, in terms of useful decision-making information, as well as enhancement tips.

It's also a good idea to work out an advertising fee with a reputable contractor who specializes in deck-building. You could also host a blog for the contractor to offer building tips and answer questions, or even accept job offers.

Taking a route like this would ensure your site an exclusive web presence with unlimited earning potential.

Peggy Hatchet

A company is judged by the president it keeps.

Are You a Writer?

One of the most difficult chores for writers is sifting through countless writing-related websites available in search of the gems that prove to be a valuable use of your time. For more than a decade, individuals have been busy scouring the Web, rummaging through every online resource imaginable in search of the very best writing resources.

Before we go any further, it's important to emphasize the red flags of *content mills* (sites like *Constant Content* and *Hubpages*) that get paid for placing ads on your work; but you might get a couple of dollars. Do not waste your time on these sites. They will rip off your work and leave you frustrated.

The best way to be compensated for your work is to host a blog and use no advertising (at first). Since you're a retiree, your income is steady enough that you can afford not to crowd your blog with annoying popups.

Establish your blog. Make it a point to post every day. Choose one subject or theme for your blog; this distinguishes you as an authority on your topic. Good, unique and interesting content guarantees search traffic.

After a while, you'll be approached by an advertiser. There's nothing more gratifying than a company wanting to put their brand on your writing.

If you choose not to wait for advertising. You can apply for Adsense placement on your blog, after blogging consistently for a couple of months. The key is NOT to worry about placing ads. Just write.

Whatever your writing fancy, the point is to do what makes you happy. When you're happy doing a thing, nothing else matters as much.

Writers are valuable to every culture.

Great Writing Resources

Bulwer-Lytton Fiction Contest
bulwer-lytton.com
Can you recall ever winning an award for writing something so terrible that it was good? That's exactly the challenge offered up by the Bulwer-Lytton Fiction Contest.

Association of Authors' Representatives
aaronline.org
The AAR is the next best thing to an accredited membership organization for literary agents, and its site allows you to search for reputable representation, read the canon of ethics AAR members have pledged to follow, and more.

The Story Starter
thestorystarter.com
With more than 1.6 billion opening lines loaded into its database, this site offers up enough ideas to last a lifetime—or at least get you through your toughest writing droughts. This way, you'll never linger in a blocked state.

Writing.com
writing.com
It's no surprise so many writers have made themselves at home on Writing.com, where you'll be amazed at how much you can do for free. You can do everything from share your work, enter contests, join writing circles and participate in a number of other writing-related activities. You even get your own Writing.com email address!

Writer Beware Blog
accrispin.blogspot.com
This industry watchdog group keeps writers and publishing professionals alike up to date on the latest scams, hoaxes and schemes circulating around the industry.

Preparing for & Surviving Natural Disasters

#8

This is another profitable niche that people find beneficial. However, for this niche to succeed, perhaps using the worst natural disasters of the past ten years as a platform for the service you offer.

Take the European heat wave of 2003, for instance. This phenomenon led to heat-related deaths, drought and food shortage. A niche site based on this disaster would include how to remain cool in deadly heat; how to store water for emergencies; emergency food storage; portable first aid kit; etc.

This niche will also benefit from things like offering a list of local storm shelters, local agencies such as Red Cross and Salvation Army; emergency numbers, emergency phone apps, reputable insurance companies, as well as the unethical ones, etc.

You could also include a Facebook app on the site for families affected by the storm to post their situation in real time. You could even partner with local rescue units, receive and post updates as they come in.

Properly executed, this vision could consistently gross hundreds of thousands of dollars annually. Seasons are constant, each of which has at least one life-threatening natural incident.

A man or woman who doesn't like serving others should continue working for others.

Peggy Hatchet

With the Internet, you can do business all over the globe, without leaving home.

Lessons (in your area of expertise)

#9

Let's say you're a great seamstress or tailor. Creating a website to offer sewing lessons would generate quite a bit of extra revenue.

This niche would require a training fee of ninety-nine dollars for a 6-month course, for example. A person seeking lessons would consider that a great deal.

For the site to be effective, you would need to have video examples of each lesson. For instance, if today's lesson is on sewing darts, students will have a visual example to accompany their written instructions.

In addition, the instructor can hold a monthly video conference to do a review of that month's lesson. Students can also submit any questions they have.

Upon completion of the course, you can give each student a certificate that documents their achievements.

Operating this niche site just right will draw attention from several major companies that will want to advertise their products, which will pull in additional money. After all, you want a moneymaking site, right?

Believe you can, and you will. Believe you will, and you shall.

Party Planner

#10

We generally love having and attending parties. There's something about a festive atmosphere that generates positive energy. And though people complain, moan and groan a lot, we prefer the lightness of positive energy over gloominess.

Planning parties of any size is fun and exciting. A person who loves planning events is always looking for ways to throw the party of the century.

You would think Martha Stewart has this niche all wrapped up, but she doesn't. There is always room for one more approach to a niche, as long as it's fresh, interesting and contagious. It has to be contagious!

Having said that, it will help to promote some of your own party creations, i.e. custom invitations, custom wine bows, place mats, etc.

If you have a party planning service of your own, that's even better. This way, your presentation is more credible. People let their guards down with the ventures they feel good about.

Money is plentiful in this niche. Every month a birthday for thousands, if not millions, of individuals.

In business, state what you do, and do what you state.

Dog Owner Info Site

#11

OMG! Money made from this niche is unthinkable, according to an acquaintance who has a dog walking business. She says her website generates a steady stream of income from dog food ads. Her website also has a visitor registration form that adds them to her database of customers and potential customers.

As an added bonus for her site visitors, she allows them to submit dog health questions. On a biweekly basis, the local veterinarian, she partners with answers their questions on dog health.

Using this idea as a model, a person could easily take a focused dog-related topic, such as healthy vaccination practices, grooming tools, best dogs for senior citizens, etc. There are many things you could do with this type of venture.

Know what will make this really take off? Dog-loving dog owners are the best candidates for this niche. First, they love dogs, which is the foundation for a successful run.

If you don't particularly care for owning a dog, don't bother considering this niche as an online moneymaking concept. Simply doing research and posting paragraphs of technical information is not enough to secure a solid place in the business. This niche is for dog lovers only.

When two men in business always agree, one of them is unnecessary.

How to Join the FBI

#12

This niche is a great project for a retired agent, who knows and loves the business. A retired FBI agent could develop the site as a pre-application process, by listing a set of qualifications or prerequisites for aspiring agents.

It could also be a resource site, which contains the history of the Federal Bureau of Investigation, its role and rank in government and so forth.

Another option would be to make this a paid membership site or do a six-month course for a flat fee.

One relevant advertiser is good for this site, probably guns or wireless transmitting devices used by federal agents.

Like the dog-owner niche, this idea will work successfully for a retired agent, who knows the protocol and holds it in a positive light.

Want ads for federal agents don't appear in local papers, however, there are hundreds of thousands of individuals who would love to know if they qualify to apply.

Remember. This niche is exclusive to retired FBI agents.

If it costs nothing, it's worth nothing.

How to Save, While Making Minimum Wage

#13

No doubt, those over 50 have a lot to say about doing more with less. However, over-crowding of this niche is no secret. Everywhere you turn, there's a financial website talking about stocks, investments and budgets.

Choosing this niche means finding the right fit, otherwise, it will have a place among the thousands of other boring sites that say the same thing about saving money.

Retired bankers, financial analysts and brokers are best suited for the technical end, but they probably have no experience being a high school dropout having to save money while working for minimum wage.

On the other hand, blue-collar workers having to work a lifetime for minimum wage and still managed to pull themselves out of poverty are by far more qualified to be successful in this niche.

Millions of families continue to struggle through financial hardships and would love to learn methods of disciplined saving, while working a low-paying job to sustain a family of three or more.

This is a rewarding niche when you find the right fit.

Peggy Hatchet

A man parting with his money expects to get what he pays for, no matter how small or great it is.

Considering an Online Business?

Managing An Online Business is as serious as managing a storefront on Main Street. It requires the same amount of diligence and attention to detail. The major difference separating the two is the Internet's global reach.

Local businesses are limited to the immediate vicinity unless they establish a unique and commanding Internet presence, where their goods and services can reach a global market.

Online businesses are operated from wherever there's an Internet connection and of course a computer with above-average systems. You can conduct business from your den, your dining room table, your home office, your patio or poolside, during family vacations.

Many potential online entrepreneurs neglect diligence, discipline and consistency because they are deceived by the term 'home-based business'.

A Point to remember: *It's easy to confuse an Internet business with recreation. Working from home is an acquired taste.*

Working from home can be a second wind for over-50 retirees.

Why Online Niche Sites Fail

An online business can only be as good as its owner. In the words of Janis Joplin, *"Don't compromise yourself. You're all you've got."* **The chief reason for online niche failure is compromise.** Some individuals compromise their priorities, their service and their business ethics. When this happens, failure is inevitable.

Most Internet startups begin with a dynamite concept; it may even have a flawless business plan and an enthusiastic creator. But if unethical practices dominate the interaction between company and consumer, this is a compromise.

Compromise destroys the exchange of genuine goods and services delivery, which is the practice that promotes consumer satisfaction. Without consumer satisfaction, consumer loyalty cannot exist. And without consumer loyalty, the business fails.

Your name is attached to the business you promote. When a business is labeled a *ripoff* and becomes known as the stay-away-from thing, people are not staying away from the business per se. They're staying away from you, the business owner.

Online businesses that are successful are ethical in business practices, remembering that defrauding and offending the client leads to eventual shutdown.

Evergreen niche markets for online business

Peggy Hatchet

Choosing a Niche

Choose a niche in which you have experience; not to mention, it helps to also like your business specialty. Entrepreneurs, who have experience in their area of endeavor, are likely to enjoy it; and an enjoyable business usually succeeds.

Decide whether you want to have a few sales trickle in once or twice a month. Or if you want a thriving niche website with loyal subscribers.

If you're one of the conscientious few, who do what's necessary to launch and run a moneymaking website, I have every confidence that you'll achieve more than you ever imagined.

Making money is the easy part. The real work lies is in the planning, organizing and the launching of a moneymaking site. The rest is merely reaping the benefits from your hard work.

The next section lists more moneymaking niche markets, along with more suggestions, strategies and procedures for making money, using your talents and the passion for what you love.

For the wise businessman, solving a problem is the first priority.

Peggy Hatchet

Evergreen Niche

Weight-Loss Regimen

An evergreen niche is one that will always be relevant. It's been around for decades and will remain a viable Internet business niche. Humans are vain and egotistical, which means they want to look good. Looking good for some merely involves losing a few pounds.

You could begin by doing reviews of different weight loss products. This can be combined with sending out weekly reviews to your subscribers, recommending safe, healthy weight-loss options.

If you're an authority on natural living or supplemental health, you could write and market an eBook as well. Your subscribers will be eager to read the book, as well as be impressed by your obvious knowledge on the subject.

If you're not a writer, and want to take the affiliate route, you can promote select products from Clickbank, Share a Sale and other reputable affiliate sources.

Since this is an evergreen niche, you will always have an income opportunity with this endeavor.

Supple, Ageless Skin

Women generally worry about their skin between 30 and 60 years of age. They experience different levels of hormone shifting at different periods in this age frame. Since all women want to look and feel beautiful, any venture promoting youthful skin sparks interest.

Promoting this site has certain vibes of energy attached to it. You get to do things like send skin revitalizing tips to subscribers, review skin care products, and video individuals talking about how well a particular skin care regimen works for them.

Hair Therapy for Thinning Hair

Both men and women have this in common. Some individuals don't have to worry about thinning hair; however, most do.

You can use a method similar to the ageless skin or the weight-loss niche. Both are concerns for aging individuals, and sometimes age isn't a factor. Whether it's stress or vitamin deficiency, thinning hair is a common occurrence in both genders.

The same rule applies. Send weekly newsletters with useful information on causes of thinning hair, how to treat it, etc. You could even review leading products, listing pros and cons. Doing a video interview of someone who uses or used the product is always a plus.

Also, if you're successfully treating a thinning hair crisis, your story is the most valuable of all.

When deciding on an angle for this niche, just remember that this niche appeals to both men and women, which means traffic will be twice as much as a gender specific niche. Your information must address both male and female hair issues.

Heading a business venture is not for everyone. The sanctity of supply and demand depends on respect for the consumer as well as the practice itself.

Your Online Niche Venture

Now that you have a sense of what Internet options are available to you, maybe you feel more optimistic about online ventures. Like other retirees who are over 50, it's easy to fall into a dark frame of mind about where you are in life.

We're indirectly taught to prepare to die when we're over 50. Retiring from decades of hard work means you can now look toward enjoying the life you worked to prepare for. However, for most, being retired means empty days spent longing for that manual labor job you were so glad to get away from.

You may not be computer savvy, and if that's the case, now you have the space to take a computer night class at your local community college. You'll be shocked to see that you're not the only mid-lifer reaching for higher goals.

Renewing your view of life, changing the way you view yourself and taking the steps necessary to take you where your dreams lead--these are the adjustments we should make at fifty something.

Speaking of fifty something, it's a marvelous life space, half a century. Think about that. If you're fifty something, you've been on our planet half a century! For most of us, many years from around 18 to about 50 or 60, our life belonged to employers, loan companies, casinos and mortgage lenders. We had no life.

Most of us are (or want to be) debt-free at 50 something. In other words, this is the life space when we are (should be) free of all material bondage.

That said, this book of amazing possibilities is my gift to you. Thank you for reading it.

To live is the rarest thing in the world. Most people live in a state of hopeless existence, because they have limiting beliefs.

The Author & the Book

 Peggy is a southern woman with universal appeal--a writer with a truth-sharing agenda.

She uses her creativity- singing, songwriting, filmmaking; journalism and photography-- to describe situations and circumstances of growing up and how to survive them.

How to Make Money Online When You're Over 50 is not part of the acclaimed *Teen Survival Series*; however, it is just as dominant in its category.

This book details niches and procedures she either researched or experienced over a period of eighteen years, and is dynamically written, poised and to the point.

Peggy Hatchet is an authentic writer who pens from the soul— a modern literary who appreciates the magic of words. Though her written word is often raw and controversial, when read, they are also instructional, enlightening and liberating.

Notes

Notes